Meet Me Halfway

Also by Samantha King Holmes

Born to Love, Cursed to Feel
Born to Love, Cursed to Feel Revised Edition
Don't Tell Me Not to Ask Why
We Hope This Reaches You in Time
She Fits Inside These Words
Anywho, I Love You

Meet Me Halfway

Samantha King Holmes

Andrews McMeel
PUBLISHING®

Andrews McMeel Publishing
a division of Andrews McMeel Universal
1130 Walnut Street, Kansas City, Missouri 64106

www.andrewsmcmeel.com

24 25 26 27 28 SDB 10 9 8 7 6 5 4 3 2 1

ISBN: 978-1-5248-9005-6

Library of Congress Control Number: 2024935827

Editor: Patty Rice
Art Director: Holly Swayne
Production Editor: Elizabeth A. Garcia
Production Manager: Julie Skalla

ATTENTION: SCHOOLS AND BUSINESSES
Andrews McMeel books are available at quantity discounts with bulk
purchase for educational, business, or sales promotional use. For information,
please e-mail the Andrews McMeel Publishing Special Sales Department:
sales@amuniversal.com.

Patty, thank you for believing in me.

To those I hold so dear, thank you for finding your way back to me. And to everyone who has been there for me during this time, I appreciate you.

act I.

Life Before

scene 3

I know we like to believe things last forever.
The truth is, it doesn't always work out that way.
I won't be mad; I won't cry.
However many seasons I get to be in your life,
I will be grateful for.
At least I got to be a part of it.

scene 4

It'll be perfect.
The day when I can think of you
Without feeling entitled to your essence.
This access has twisted our connection.

I've binged on your dreams, your hopes,
Your beliefs, the driving force behind you.
I know your preferences and the echoes of your fears,
Even the unspoken ones, universal in nature.

Except if you fall, your crash would be seen,
And others would stand at the fire,
Arms extended, phone in hand, to document.
Some would feign empathy, while others would revel.
All would want attention to themselves
Over how they felt about what happened to you.

I don't know you.
I shouldn't assume I do.
I mean no offense,
But I'm yearning to
No longer care about you
And what you're doing,
Or how you've been,
Or what comes next.

Frankly, in my life,
Nothing that happens in yours
Matters in mine.
I've just been given a window
That I no longer wish to look into.

I hope by the time I get to the end of this,
That saying goodbye to you
Won't seem so impossible.

I wish you well.

scene 5

It's hard being here sometimes,
Endlessly toiling away in my mind.
What am I running from?
Sometimes, without explanation or warning,
Tears come, my face stained with the journey of their existence.

Then I'm off again,
Chasing down the thought of some knight
Coming to save me.
But he can't remove me from myself.
So where are we going?

scene 6

I miss connection,
Laughing till our stomachs cramped,
Dancing till sweat dripped down our backs,
Feeling like we could take on the world
Because it was us against it.

I miss feeling safe,
Confessing my sins as if you could absolve me,
Knowing they wouldn't ever pass from your lips
To someone else's ears.

I miss feeling like I wasn't alone,
Journeying through the dark.

I miss friendship,
Holding you while you cried,
Always only a call away,
Never having to question your loyalty.

I miss it.
What I mean to say is I miss you.

scene 7

I bought your favorite cookies
For a hit of nostalgia.
Except they tasted like nothing.
Not like home
Or your warm hugs.
Not the least bit of your laughter
Or the way you always made sure I felt loved.
Not of our happy times
Or even the bad ones.

I was hoping they would do something more.
Transport me back to a time
When things made more sense.
But there was nothing.
Now I'm just stuck missing everything.

scene 8

As your friend,
I have your love forever.
If I were anything more,
You would pick me apart,
For the love of the romantics demands perfection,
While the love of friends merely asks for acceptance.

So, you will love me forever,
Knowing nothing of my morning breath
Or occasional obsessive behavior.
No, you will be allotted a lifetime of my devotion,
My awkward yet charming mannerisms,
And my unyielding gratitude

For granting me space to be myself
And refuge when that's hard to do.

scene 212

Similar in so many ways, not just in our names.
A bond that's transcended distance and time.
My favorite soulmate.
Always there to be my guiding light.
Not ever alone with you by my side.
Through the toughest of times, we've held true.
How fortunate life saw fit to give me a friend like you.
A testament to the love that sustains.

My dear, sweet Samantha, you are everything.

scene 902

Your chest heaves
As life has dealt you another blow.
We always think we're out of the woods
When, really, we're building the armor
Life feels we need to have.

You are a champion in the making,
My dear, sweet friend.
Your faith, while shaken, is still intact.
Unwavering in that there is another side
To this current tribulation.

And I am never too far away
To be the comfort you need, to make you laugh.
It's not for me to take this away.
I am but a companion.
Fortunate enough to cross your path.

You must see yourself through this.
And you will.
I'll be watching.
Just in case you need a place to lean
As you find your way out.

scene 9

Sometimes, we focus so much on the dream
We have in our minds of how our lives should be
That we forget to appreciate the way it is.

scene 10

What is my body holding onto?
What emotions are ingrained deep in the tissues,
Wrapped around my muscle memory?

What history has seeped into my bones?
Rattling around like ghosts with a grudge
They can't relinquish.

What have I been dragging around every corner,
Hoping things will be different,
Not realizing they can't be
If I'm still the same.

scene 11

The passion,
So fickle, so fleeting.
What it feeds is so small,
It doesn't fill the space.
It doesn't stick;
Just makes room for more
Cravings to replace it.

Their lips and tongue
Are unable to hold
The truth in your name.
They've tasted too many lies.
Their palettes are tainted.
They don't know how to savor you.
So, they mindlessly devour,
Hoping you're the cure to everything
They're missing.

scene 12

Bartering the most precious parts of ourselves
For a bit of company.
Hoping someone latches on,
Only for them to retreat.
"Fleeting" does no justice to the brevity
Of these fruitless interactions.

Have we devolved so much
We don't see the soul
Inside the being?
Just what they have to offer
With nothing to spare for them.

scene 13

We are so unforgiving of ourselves.
Others can trespass on our bodies,
Our souls, our intentions,
And they're extended grace.
Hell, they get an invitation back.

Our inner critics are relentless, never at ease.
We scrutinize our actions, words, and flaws,
Yet, in this quest for self-improvement, we find no peace,
While we offer pardons to others, making them whole.

scene 14

I recognized something in you
That you weren't saying.
It was your loneliness.

I called out to you,
But you didn't hear me.
I hope you find this instead,
And know you're not alone.

I saw you. I see you.
Yes, you're worth loving.

I wish I could have been some solace
Or extended a kind word.
I let the moment slip out of my grasp,
Recognizing myself in you stopped me in my tracks.

From my soul to yours,
I hope you find what you're looking for.

scene 15

I hope that, despite the clouds,
You always know something better
On the other side is waiting for you.

I hope that disappointments in life
Never keep you down longer than they should.

I hope you don't get weighed down by expectations
And rise to the occasion of your greatness on your terms.

I hope what they say about you doesn't ever stick.
Let it roll off and meet its demise beneath you.

I hope that if you ever question my love for you
That you know my answer will be the same today
As it will be tomorrow:
"Always."

scene 16

O, sweet joy, you are like
The cherry blossoms that bloom in spring.
You arrive full, radiant and overwhelming,
Petals sweetly graze my skin,
Filling me with abundant laughter.
Then, just like that, you're gone,
Withering to nothing more than
Remnants scattered on the ground.
You are now just a picturesque memory.
Here I remain, waiting for spring to come again.

scene 17

The sweet melodies of whispered secrets,
Late mornings spent with fingertips tracing words on backs,
Long strolls to destinations unknown,
An intimacy that transcends words.
What have we so willingly sacrificed?

Endorphin bursts so brief, we chase them endlessly.
Once, people were adventures to be explored.
Now, their stories lie bare for all to see.
There is no anticipation, no buildup, no mystery,
Just a waning desire for connection that dwindles.

scene 18

Skin to skin, yet no connection forms.
Our spirits remain unentwined.

Deep dives,
Not to the places I want you to explore,
Only the ones you can handle.
What are you searching for in me?
My body is not a solace from your trauma.
I can't love you into treating me with care,
And yet I let you come to the altar
And bear your pain the only way you know how to.

Am I breaking myself apart to heal you?
That's not my charge in life.
I just don't have it in me to abandon you.
I've given all I can into not needing you too.
My soul can only bear so much redemption.

scene 19

I have to figure out
How to stop you from being
A specter in my thoughts,
Following me from daydream to daydream,
Making every waking moment about you.

Have I made obsessing over you a habit,
Awestruck by the mere entertainment of your existence?

Your name tickles my lips
As it escapes out of my mouth.
Please stop.
I don't love you.
Please stop.
I need a reprieve.
Please stop.
I know you wouldn't ever choose me.

scene 20

I know what love looks like.
I even know its taste, bittersweet.
You never forget how warm it feels
As it flows, intoxicating.

I know what it smells like.
Its scent lingers on my sheets.
I know its touch, its laugh.
I've even been blessed to hear its heartbeat.

I know love.
Sometimes, I just feel it doesn't know me.

scene 21

I'd rather talk about love.
Pain has known me too well.
I'd rather give voice to the hope of forever,
To the softness of skin and spirit.

I'd rather talk about those sleepless nights,
Dreaming about you with my eyes open,
And the ones when your voice keeps me awake.
Being under the same sky, not enough.
Don't tell me I've gotten this close to happiness
Only to be so far away from it.

I want to talk about desire
And the thrill of anticipation,
About the mundaneness of the day-to-day
And how I wouldn't trade that for anything.

scene 22

I'm looking for a love story to call my own,
Borrowing others' as a means of escape.
I feel out of place. I get it wrong so often.
They come up short, minor characters,
The harm they cause cataclysmic.

I yearn for a moment of reprieve from the pain.
I give so much and gain so little.

Could you maybe love me again?
This time, better, kinder, truer.

scene 23

What if I grow to hate your laugh?
Or the way you chew your food?
I'm asking myself all this
While you inch your way to me.

Can I really expect forever in a moment?
Captivated by the allure of your brown eyes,
There's just something about you
That I can't quite get out right.

Then you say, "Hello."
(I'm yours.)

scene 24

Run away with me.
Don't look back.
Not at what you've been through,
Not at whom you've loved.

Just come away with me.
Let's get lost in each other,
Under the cover of the stars,
Wounds still raw to the touch.

Don't make any promises.
Not that your love will heal me.
Not that you have any of the answers.
Not that this will even last.

Just be here with me, truly.
Let's see what that looks like.

scene 25

I could get lost in daydreams about you.
So, I do.
I let myself be devoured.
You love me passionately.
I'm encapsulated by your smile.

We talk for hours on end.
Nothing, everything, and whatever falls in between.
You laugh when I'm awkward, but not at me,
In that way that lets me know that you adore me,
Even when I forget some of the lyrics and sing off-key.

It's these moments when I lose myself in you,
When I know I can love you devoutly,
There isn't a moment I don't want to spend with you
In this house that I've built in my mind,
Constantly learning, always curious.

I let you break my heart, too,
Let myself feel the devastation,
The betrayal of not being loved as is,
Feeling like a stranger,
Distant, so far from the person
Whose eyes drew me and have kept me since.
I let you break my heart.

This is all in my head,
A fairy tale, a tragedy,
As if life itself
Doesn't live somewhere between the two.
I guess I prepare myself for either ending.
I just know that I want to know you.

scene 26

When you rest your head, do thoughts of me bloom?
Do you nurture them, allowing them to flourish?
Till all you see is me and endless possibilities?

It started as just one.
Now there's a whole field dedicated to you,
Growing wild and free in my mind.

Now, I see you in everything.
Is this love or just a product of my imagination?

scene 27

Life, with its twists and turns,
And us,
Masters of our fates.
Or are we all merely tracing each line
Within a preordained script?
Are these our steps
Or the ones we were charged with taking?

First dates, core memories,
Our longing, our pain,
Desires, vices, virtues, redemption:
Destiny or our decisions?
Would our love for life diminish?
Would you feel any less like mine if we were told it's fate?

Would we still be friends?
If you knew that someone handpicked me
To stand by your side
And follow through whatever journey
They had laid out for us?
Would anything change?
Or would we convince ourselves
That control is an illusion but we are still free?

act II.

Life During

scene 912

How did it take you so long to find your way back?
Did the world, in its vast knowledge and wisdom,
Feed you plenty?
Did you bring anything back to share with me?
Did the love you found without me last,
Or was I tucked away in a nook, always transcending?

Your voice is spellbinding.
I can barely catch my breath.
Please speak no lies.
I have so little faith left.

How long were you gone?
Time must be mistaken.
It feels like none has passed.

We are still those kids.
Will you finally hold my hand?
I have so much to tell you,
Something like a dream.

I'm sure you already know this,
That's all life really is,
A soul dreaming.

scene 111

Take me back
To my fingers dancing along your right shoulder,
Your hand rubbing my left thigh.
Somewhere between bliss and anxiety.
I didn't let anything stop me from seeing you
And those beautiful green eyes.

Take me back
To your stubble rubbing against my neck.
Could you feel how hard my pulse was beating?
Did you lean in to hear the music my body played
As a welcome to this meeting?

Whiskey sours, shy glances, hand-holding
With fingers intertwined.
Like a signal to anyone watching
That, for now, you're all mine.

Streetlights, cold walk, and could you hold me a little tighter?
I know this night is coming to an end.
I'm doing what I can to prolong it.

This is the best date I've ever had.
Don't tell anyone.
Everyone thinks they're special.
You actually are.

scene 415

Journeying through life, hand in hand.
Affectionate moments, so tender and dear.
Seasons change, yet our bond remains.
One look from you and my heart still flutters.
Nothing has ever compared, or ever will.

scene 28

With you, I don't want to be patient.
I want to dive right in.
Can we get to the part where I wake up
To kisses on my shoulder?

How about the long walks with no destination in mind?
The adventures, the endless nights of laughing,
whiskeys neat, and your hand playing in mine.

Old buildings, cobblestone streets.
Nights away from each other seeming too long.
The moments I daydream about you.
The times you look at your phone, hoping it's me.

I know I shouldn't rush.
It's just, I need to know
If there is heartbreak down this road,
Or could this be something more?

scene 29

I know I should slow down,
But my feet haven't touched the ground
Since that first time your lips touched mine.
Don't mind me if I get carried away.

I have no anchor here.
Simply hoping life won't veer me off course.
It led me to your path,
So maybe there's something to that.

Your eyes dancing in my mind
And the touch of your hand on my face,
Taking up all the space it can.
I won't ask for eternity yet, just honesty.

My heart's been dragged around too many times,
And I'm trying not to be terrified
That you're giving me something to believe in.

scene 30

It's always been electric with you.
Nerves shooting off like fireworks,
I try not to get too lost in your words.
Did you know then?
That the way I feel about you
Doesn't feel like it has a name?
How are my laughs so awkward?
Don't try to hold my hand; it's too sweaty.

When it's 1am and you can't sleep
Do you miss me the way I do you?
Are you tempted to call?
Just to hear me smiling on the other end?
You've always been home for me.
All you needed to say was, "Come back."

scene 31

It's 5:31am.
I've been up daydreaming about you.
I don't know if this is happiness, love, or a possibility.
I'm just doing my best not to run from
The sense of comfort you give,
The warmth of your gaze,
And the tingly sensation I get
When you kiss my forehead.

scene 32

If I tell you I miss you,
Would that be too much?
Cause there's no denying
My skin misses your touch.
Firm hugs and gentle kisses,
Our spirits kindred.
What did I do to deserve you?

The way you look at me stirs
This desire for exploration.
Go on this journey with me.
Think nothing of expiration.
Just hand yourself over;
Let's see what happens.
If I map out the way to my heart,
Don't take advantage.

scene 33

I wonder if anyone looks at you
With love the way I do.
I doubt they can.
They don't have my eyes for you.
The way they scan your soul,
Finding a way to the center of you.

They don't know your hands the way I do.
Not in the traces they make on skin,
The safety found in your embrace,
Or the mark your touch leaves behind.

I have always been yours.
Will you ever be mine?

scene 34

Right now, you're asleep.
And I'm just missing you.
Too far for your touch to graze my skin
As you fidget in bed.
Beyond the reach of your body's warmth.
Your breath can't touch my face
As I try to nuzzle mine under your chin.
Limbs aren't entwined in a mad dance
Of comfort, love, and a need to be that much closer.

I am playing the recording you sent last Tuesday.
So I can hear your voice before I go to sleep.
Find me in a dream; this distance is crushing me.

scene 35

You find me in my dreams.
I awake to you saying my name.
Be with me always like this,
Wrapped in warmth and truth.

You found your way back to me.
It's been so long.
That doesn't matter.
We pick up where we left off.
What does our story still hold to tell?

scene 36

I won't say those three words too soon.
Instead, I'll offer you this.

I've stared fondly into pools of hazel.
Enchanted by the reflection.
I could stay there all day in solitude
With those mesmerizing glimpses into the soul.
Coconspirators in unfurling my heart.

The charming gatekeepers of untold pleasure.
That continually take me in.
Soft whispers of affection.
Cascading over every inch in need of nourishment.

Speak to me.
Speak my name.
So that I know I am yours only.

Those versatile sculptors of your intentions
Have reached places no one has ever entered.
And that no one else will.
For you alone am I this way.

Do you get it yet?
This time, will you stay?

scene 37

Are you toying with me or is that longing on your breath?
Tell me of your desires, slowly.
I want to absorb everything.

Hold me again.
I'm yearning for the softness of your lips on my forehead.
Your arms caged around my ribs.
A feeling of both safety and passion.

You once told me that being loved by you felt like heaven.
I need you to come back and open the gates.
I'm ready to walk through.
(Wherever this leads with you.)

scene 38

My thoughts run wild with your face and that smile.
I've been trying to decipher the connection,
Why you roam my mind like you're already mine.
I've asked the universe,
I've asked my dreams.
I can't ask you,

Cause you would hear it in the way I breathe your name.
See it when my gaze falls and I smile.
It feels like I know you deeply,
As if we've shared more than just words.
My soul knows it, knows you.
I want to tell you everything,
I just can't yet.

I'm scared to listen to your voice.
Afraid I won't want to stop.
It's stirring this passion in me to know you,
Clumsily falling over my feelings.

If I told you I loved you,
You'd probably think I was lying,
But there is a happiness that pervades
Anytime I'm in your space.

I'll leave it all here,
Cause I just can't tell you yet.

scene 39

If I wrote about you as much as I thought about you,
There would be volumes dedicated to your touch alone.
Heaven forbid I dive into the cascading sultriness of your voice.
Days would be reserved to capturing the warmth you've exuded.

Does that fall in line with touch?
Maybe, but it deserves so much more than a footnote.
Right now, in my mind, I'm beckoning you to hug me again.
It's the place I truly feel I belong to, belong in.
Safe, beloved.

Now, your eyes,
Gazing into them feels like an intimacy too sacred to share.
So, I'll keep that for myself.

"I love you" doesn't feel like enough anymore.
Thank you for finding me.
Now, don't let go.

scene 40

Most days, I'm exhausted, crestfallen,
Sleep-deprived, and yearning.
I still find time to love you.

scene 41

It's hard to watch someone else's love story
While you're waiting for your own.
You find yourself counting their blessings.
While yours lay forgotten.

In my life,
I get left behind.
That's the weight of pity.
A tether to my soul, pulling me back
To everything I can't let go of.

scene 42

Are you yearning the way I am?
I don't understand it, the silence.
How can you just float through it,
Unmarred by any desire to hear me say your name?
It's madness, your resolve, and my lack of composure.
How can you bear the distance
That's growing larger by the second?
Is this some test to see if my passion is true?
Or am I a fool who read too much into things?
I want you. I know that.
Do you want me is the question.

I won't chase after affection.
So, tell me plainly,
If loving you is beyond reach
Then I need space to forget you.

scene 43

I didn't sleep well, even with you beside me.
I'm always blamed, demeaned, ridiculed.
I'm exhausted.
Always giving in after every fight,
Trying to appease despite being right.

Your words have lost their meaning,
Paling against actions that contradict them.
How sad it seems you don't even know me at all.
Tell me again, how is it that you came to love me?

scene 44

We started keeping score; you hurt me,
So I needed to return the blow.
Enough was never truly enough.

Most days were easy, bad days, nightmarish.
The smallest thing would send us into a downward spiral.
You rarely apologized first.
I would always crawl back up beside you.
A piece of me ticked away every time.

People stopped telling us apart.
You never saw the problem with that.
You didn't have to live in your shadow.
At times, it was lonely there.

And I would let you pick me up,
Dust me off and make me feel special.
You spent so much time trying to fix others.
You didn't fix me.
No one did, not even me.

scene 45

First, it was just a fray.
Then, there were several.
I could hear the tear begin.
Where's the needle?
What am I sewing us up with this time?

Am I in denial?
Is this tear too big?
Why are you just standing there staring?
Look at what we did.
What we've done.

What we always do. Come apart.
We need something to patch it.
I've given so much of myself.
Can I get something from you this time?
I'll give a bit more if it happens again.

scene 46

The way we fight now
Is building callus on my heart.
Or maybe it's my soul.
Either way, there's damage.
You have to know that.
You make me not want to
Ever know anyone else this well.

scene 47

Resolutions linger somewhere
Outside the spectrum of our patience.
You're mad again.
It's my fault, always is.
I'm the problem,
Or so I've been led to believe.

We must discuss your feelings,
My transgressions against you.
Anything that happens to me
Is lost in your need to move forward.
I am merely an afterthought
You like to have around who listens.

You've spared me nothing.
You wouldn't be lost without me.
You would barely even notice.

scene 48

I know you heard me crying.
Words must have failed you.
A hug couldn't mend the gap.
So you relied on silence to stitch up the wound.

scene 49

When did you stop wanting to explore me?
You no longer pick my mind.
My inner workings, once your playground,
Now lay abandoned.

Our interactions have become surface level, at best.
And I'm left asking, *Where'd the passion go?*
Did I move too fast? You, too slow?
Was this ever real or just a figment of my hopes?

I'm left wanting, waiting. Knowing deep down
The version of you I'm looking for won't be coming back.
How is it that now I have to let you go
When I had no intent of letting you in?

scene 50

When I fall short, you don't meet me halfway.
So, I carry the weight till my heart hurts and my body aches.
I fight back the tears.
I'm my only hope now.

Delirious from the exhaustion,
I think I see a way out.
"I need help" sits on my tongue.
But my lips won't fix themselves to concede.

I keep going despite being so close to the brink.
You were made to get through tough days,
Is what I tell myself.

All those times I waited,
And no one showed up.
I'm not sticking around
For the disappointment this time.
I am my own hero.

scene 51

My God, the words that have escaped your lips
And seeped in to destroy me.
You revel in it, finding pleasure in
The involuntary cringe of my body.

There is no mercy left, no touch of grace.
You've witnessed my tears countless times
And didn't reach out to comfort me.
No hint of remorse etched on your face.
I should have discerned it then,
Whatever shreds of humanity and empathy
You reserve for others; none extend toward me.

We are not friends, we are not enemies, we are nothing.
How sad, when, once upon a time, we were everything.

scene 52

You got so caught up living in the past,
I started to live there with you.
You loved who I once was.
"She" would understand you.
It's just a subtle way
To convey that you and I no longer align.

There isn't anything left here.
We once had each other,
But I have never been more sure
I am alone in this.

No more trapeze act.
No more playing small.
No more pretending.
We've stopped saying "I love you."
How honest of us.

scene 53

The softness that was once here is gone.
Replaced by hardened resentment.
When did your heart stop holding a place for me in it?
The kindness has been stripped from your words.
My every flaw is now cataloged.
It isn't that I am not enough.
You just don't want me anymore.

scene 54

You know it's over
When you start living for the memories.
"You remember when . . ."
It's not just reminiscing.
It's an attempt to rekindle
The emotions once felt.
You've succumbed to the monotony.
Life has become all too predictable.
You're craving a spark, something refreshing,
To make this worth saving.

scene 55

Where did we place forever?
Did it roll under the couch,
Too far out of our reach?
Can we get it back somehow?

If you move this way and push,
And I move that way and pull,
Maybe we'll see it again.

You push, and I pull, no movement.
I push, and you pull, not a budge.
I ask, "Are you really even trying?"
You respond, "Of course."
You ask me the same thing.
And I look at you in a daze.
How could you ever doubt that I would?

Exhausted, we finally give in and sit.
Knowing that forever will be left
For someone else to find it.

scene 56

He's worried.
I sense it in the urgency of his kiss,
As if he needs me to know love is still here.
He's searching my eyes for an answer
That he hasn't asked.

This isn't about me but about the loss.
I am but a vessel he is desperately trying to convince to stay.
His hand glides up my back,
Presses me firmly against his chest.
A wild dance of blood and pulse.
Beating relentlessly against my stony exterior.

This isn't love; this is fear
Of what comes next,
Of what that means,
And what a world looks like
Without our steps placed firmly beside the other.

scene 57

Your pain is coming through loud and clear,
"Lost On You" scaling the walls.
The fluctuations of your pain resonate.
I'm attempting to find refuge in some corner,
Granting you space to navigate your emotions.

At times, they roar with intensity,
While others find a somber tranquility.
Recently, they've surged to new heights.
I can't tell if the rejection is hurting you more
Or if you're genuinely agonized over losing me.

scene 58

It's hard to commit to letting go.
Your affection, however infrequent now,
Is something I still long for.
The smell of your hair
While you lie on my chest.
Just you being close to me at all.
Makes it harder to just say . . . anything, really.
I'm hanging on, living for a good moment with you.
Cause it's when I feel alive, loved even.

I'm fooling myself; deep inside, I understand,
The moment I make up my mind to go,
You'll realize everything this was.
I can't sit around and wait for that.

scene 59

I've learned not to comment on how
The mood in the room has changed
Or dwell on the fact that you won't meet my eyes.
You say I don't know you; that's a lie.

I'm acquainted with every nuance,
From the subtle to the significant.
That you'll flee into another room for space,
Silently seething with righteous indignation.

There's no winning.

We've gotten better, but the cracks have grown,
Exposing flaws that we try to conceal.
Perhaps we should have taken more care.

I wonder if I brought this upon myself,
Didn't voice my needs strongly enough,
Make it evident what I would and wouldn't accept.

It appears that our path has steadily shifted.
Toward the wrong direction.
Anger surfaces swiftly these days,
While affection slowly fades.

Within the quiet of words left unexpressed, we exist.
Seeking solace in the fragments of our past.
Yet, as we confront this shifting terrain,
I question if our connection can ever last.

scene 60

I speak to you in a hushed tone,
Afraid of my own voice.
It's you who has altered how I perceive myself
And magnify that much more when you're angry.

If only someone knew,
Then maybe I would have the strength
To do what I know is right.
In my heart, I know that's a lie,
To give me a morsel of comfort,
This thought of a way out.

The reality is that this has been going on for so long.
You don't need to make excuses;
I make them for you.
I need to wake up.
Someone, please wake me up.

scene 61

Never thought you'd be the one
To have me crying in the dark.
Insecure about myself,
Unsure about us.

Never thought you'd be the one
To lie when you said,
"She's just a friend."
You haven't looked at anyone like that since me,
So how could she be just that then?

Never thought you'd be the one
To leave the way you did.
With broken promises and tattered dreams
Overflowing from the garbage.

Never thought I'd be the one
To have to start again.
But here I am.
I will survive,
I will live.
I always have.

scene 62

I can't reach you anymore.
These walls are too thick.
My voice sounds muffled,
And the sentences break apart.
Only the worst sentiments seem to reach you,
Getting trapped on the other side.
Do you even remember when it wasn't like this?

It's so quiet now in our garden.
The thorns have the loveliest roses in their grasp,
The tulips have shut themselves up.
It seems everything is afraid to bloom here,
Except for the dandelions.
I don't blame them.

I'm standing here thinking of a way in,
Wondering if I should be on the other side.

My own wall begins to grow.
Your voice now has no chance,
Reduced too far in the distance to understand.
I miss the garden.
I miss the light.
I miss when being together
Was more important than being right.
I miss it all.
(Tell me, do you?)

scene 63

I've abandoned the effort to set things right.
There is no "back to normal."
It's lost for good, this time.
I don't believe we can recover from this,
No matter how we may want to.

What hypocrites we must seem now.
I think I've always hidden you away
From the harshness of my words, spared you.
A courtesy that you have not bestowed upon me.

We've taken too much from each other,
Too much pain, too much hurt,
Not enough forgiveness.

scene 64

What did I say?
I can't even remember.
Did I mean it?
I'm sure I did.
Was it worth the price of you now feeling so distant?
No, not ever.

I used to be able to talk to you,
Didn't I?
Or was that all in my head?
I remember you fondly; it's just a feeling,
But I trust it more than anything.
So, how are we here now?
With you so far and me wanting you near?
Tell me I can make it right.
You're not someone I want to be wrong with.

scene 65

Exhausted, I yearn to unfurl underneath your wakeful eye,
Cozy up to you for comfort,
And find it tucked safely between your arm and side.
You are the serenest space I've ever gotten to call home.
Your eyes casting a trance I have no desire to retreat from.
Feed me your voice and your dreams.
I will devour them and sleep happily.

scene 66

When they ask about the end,
I'll explain it as a thousand tiny cuts.
Not some grand demise but more of a whimper.
A deflation of love that quietly hit the floor.
All of it became too much.

At one point, it existed.
And it was new and rejuvenating.
Never perfect, but nothing is.
There was friendship, conversations that seemed endless,
Jokes told in the middle of the night,
Comfortable silences, and a love that felt like it spanned lifetimes.

It still came to an end.
As all things do.
Not with a flourish.
More like the soft footfalls
Of a silent retreat.

I'll tell them there was magic.
That there were good days
And tough years.

I'll tell them that, somehow, we lost sight of us,
And none of that is their fault.

That you can have the best of intentions
And still be left baffled
By how badly things go.
That I stopped fighting the tide
And gave in to the change.

This great shift in our lives, their lives,
that flipped our world upside down.
My hands unable to swiftly catch
Every cherished thing I hold dear.
So, I let it all crash
And held on to the most important part, them.

scene 67

I won't ever forget that night on the couch.
You tried so earnestly to reach out to me,
Anything to close the distance.
Pain had already carried me so far away.

It was etched on your face, the agony.
Even that couldn't reach the shore of my self-preservation.
The look on my face must have been blank.
It was then you realized how far gone we both were.

A loss of purpose, of planning, of family, of friend.
I apologize.
To cause you any such pain wasn't anything I ever intended.
Things just got away from us.

First, the kindness between us went, followed by some respect.
The touch of grace that we needed disappeared.
By then, there was no thread.
You only ever wanted to be loved deeply.
I swear I did.

It just started to feel like it was at the expense of myself.
A price I wasn't willing to pay.
Does it always take such sacrifice?
Has it always been that way?
I really do wish you the best that happiness has to offer.

scene 68

Beautiful stranger,
What stirred my desire to know you?
Was it your plan to take my heart in your wake?
Did you always know it belonged to you?

For all the pain in your departure,
I can't deny the good you've done.
Am I selfish for seeking to fill the void you left?
Or am I that for thinking I could keep you?

You beautiful stranger,
Why couldn't you remain just that?
A fond fantasy, a lingering gaze,
Eyes met, words unspoken.

No, instead, you made me love you.
How am I to move on from this?

We started as strangers,
Fast friends, lovers,
To strangers again.

scene 69

We're all looking for a soft landing
As the inevitable crash looms.
No expiration date to brace for,
Just a budding anxiety
That every turn leads to an end, our end.

Didn't you promise forever?
Was it sincere then?
When did that start to seem too long to love me?

I'm being hard on us.
Life has been hard on us.
Will parting ways truly lighten the load?

Here we stand at this crossroads,
Caught between the echoes of promises
And the weight of reality settling in.

Letting go may not erase the hardships.
Yet, within that surrender, we might discover
The strength to face a new beginning.

act III.

Life After

scene 70

Don't let anyone tell you the type
Of strength you should have.
When you're the only one
Who feels the full impact
Of what life puts you through.

scene 71

At one point in time, I didn't think of you.
Didn't feel the need to know you.
Then, all at once, I was consumed by the thought of you.
Now, I must teach myself not to think of you all over again.
What a cruel cycle.

scene 72

There wasn't enough space
For you and everything that came before.
So, I chose you.
And was left with nothing but the void
When you took your leave.
Confronted by my choice and the price I paid for it.

scene 73

I want to break something.
For there to be a physical expression
Of how shattered I feel.

What good would that do, though?
Two broken things in a room
Unaware of how to be whole again.

scene 74

Taking a moment to silence my thoughts.
Here we go again, another spiral,
Another sea of denial.
I keep walking this shore.

Calloused feet from the journey.
I persist anyway.
Another disappointment, another betrayal,
Another exploitation.

What I'm too afraid to confess
Is that I'm looking for a way out.
And yet, I remain adrift.
What's left but to jump in?

scene 75

I will never be everything to you again.
Your capacity to love me that way is lacking.
I will never be everything to you.
I stopped wanting to live under your gaze.

You've led me to this place.
Where I no longer want to know you well.
Quite content to be displaced from being yours.
When once upon a time, I'd give anything to know you.

What was it all for?
Why did I need it so badly?
Why couldn't I see clearly back then what I see now?

You spelled trouble for me.
An ache of the heart of a different kind.
You never saw me.
That's what I've realized.

You only saw what you needed.
How sad for you.
To miss out on seeing me for who I am,
Not merely as a set of convenient attributes.

scene 76

I know nothing you say will be satisfying.
A subversion into some neat form of closure.

So, say nothing,
And let my heart break.
Say nothing,
And let me forget you.
Nothing.
You will no longer hold any
Significance in my life.
Live with that.

scene 77

Your fingers and mine interlocked in my mind
Feel like some sick joke my heart wasn't in on.
The tender words spoken in the dead of night
Now shred my sensibility to pieces.
You were sincere, weren't you?
No, a voice within quietly contradicts.

The memory of the sensation of your stubble
Against my cheek pulls me deeper.
But it's your eyes, like unwavering oceans of certainty,
That leave me questioning.
How were you so unsure about me?
Or was I just not paying attention?

 I don't want to move, scared I might fall apart.

scene 78

1am rolls around,
And thoughts of you
Call out to me like a siren.
Beckoning me to relive our demise.
The way I rushed in and the way you recoiled.

I gave myself away
When I said, "I love you."
You gave yourself away
When you said nothing.

You didn't offer me anything substantial.
It was all a product of my imagination.
Here I am, sleep eluding me,
As I endlessly replay our conversations.
Actions over words.
A truth to live by.
But words are all I have left of you.

scene 79

I miss you as deeply as trees in winter
long for the return of their lost leaves.
Their branches bare, reaching out in vain.
Aching for the embrace of spring's warmth.

I miss you like a melody yearns for its harmony,
Echoing through empty spaces, seeking completion,
Longing for the unity that only you can bring,
To weave together the symphony of my soul's song.

I hate myself for it.
The way I miss you.
It feels like a piece of me is gone.
If you're so vital, intertwined with my existence,
How are you not missing me?

scene 80

Here I am again.
Trying to find the words
To explain how much this hurts.
As I extend my hand out.
For a way to reach you.
A singular thought breaks through.
It doesn't matter.

I pull my hand back under the cover.
Wrap it around my stomach and try to console myself.
How long will I be awake this time?
Minutes, hours.
Not again, please, not again.
My mind hasn't found a way to forget you yet.

Fight to sleep, fight to rest.
My dreams are now the one place
You can't find me.
I've been spared nightmares.
Perhaps reality is harsh enough
For anything else to haunt me.

scene 81

Where did I go wrong?
With you, I felt safe, vital,
Then all those sweet nothings
Evaporated into silence.
I'm still grasping for answers.

Your hands no longer recognize beauty,
Pleasure misplaced.
Your heart, well, I can only imagine,
It's been let down.

I've begun to close all the doors.
Locking them neatly behind me.
You were it; that's enough.
I can no longer trust myself.

I'm sorry for all the ways life has disappointed you.
I will not fail myself.
There is no need to seek redemption through me.
Rather, treasure those who hold you dear.

scene 82

I run from the silence.
I feel too much when I'm alone.
What would happen if I gave in
Is a question I'm afraid to answer.

I allow myself to get lost when my curiosity piques.
Interests have a way of draining my time.

My mind isn't fond of being still,
So I fill it so the chaos outside matches the interior.

Silence, it just doesn't play fair.
It forces things out all at once.
Till the voices just drown each other out.
It's a roar.

Silence just doesn't work for me.
There's too much to extract from its depths.
Hasn't enough been taken?

scene 83

Shards of glass scraping against gray folds.
Will I ever truly be rid of you?
Or are you to follow me to the end?

Loving you was a sort of madness.
Being free of you is no less distressing.

scene 84

Is it because I feel so easily forgotten
By those who came before you?
Bearing deceit on their tongues
And promises of forever in their hands,
Nothing more than passing fancies.
Was I ever meant to be more than that to someone?
I wanted to be regaled, revered, madly loved.

Why do I need you to love me so badly?
More importantly, how do I make it stop?

scene 85

My heart feels like a mausoleum.
For all the versions of me
Who lived to feel loved.
Sometimes, I visit, leaving flowers.
The sole mourner of those past selves,
The solitary voice that tries to penetrate the stone.
I am the only one who ever truly loved them.

scene 86

Where do I begin?
Where does the stench of inner turmoil lead?
I've been searching for the roots.
Unearthing fragments of myself intertwined with echoes of you,
Some from them; others, I'm still figuring out.

What a waste of time avoidance has been.
Freedom was always on the other side of the pain.
The only way out was to acknowledge it, not abolishment.
All this time, I've been hating parts of myself
When all I needed was to understand the moments of their creation.

I will accept all parts.
I will acknowledge all parts.
I will love all parts, always.

scene 87

My eyes are heavy.
My soul, restless.
My thoughts, a wandering tide,
Ebbing and flowing toward you.

I've almost done it.
Released myself from the bondage
Of thinking about you tirelessly every day.
Are you free of me yet?

I am tired and lonely.
What comfort are my thoughts
When all they lead back to are memories?

Days when I felt loved,
Times when I felt seen,
Held securely in an embrace.
Caressed tenderly, kissed passionately.

Only to be reminded that this is my reality.
I am tired and lonely,
Wishing to feel like everything to someone all over again.

scene 88

I still write to you,
Cause there's no one else
I want to share my love with.

scene 818

I can still hear it.
The crunch of the snow under our feet.
Your comforting presence walking beside me.
I remember feeling safe as you drove through the storm.
You brought me to your home; you let me in.
This is how we began.

We didn't know it then,
What we would come to mean to one another.
Listening to music in your car while we talked.
We would revisit us for years to come.
Neither of us asked the other to stay.

You taught me so much about myself.
I wasn't what you needed then.
Although, my life, you changed.
You still remain to be the kindest
In the way you said goodbye.

If it is true that you get three loves in your life,
You would be the first of mine.
I didn't tell you that then.
Just that I would love you always.
I meant it.

scene 407

Thank you for loving me the way you did.
I should have never let you go.
No one has captured my heart the way you did.
It's taken me far too long to comprehend that.
There was something pure about us, sacred.

I think life spun you round.
Now, the optimist I adored
Is someone who looks at life for everything it's not.
You don't like the hand you were dealt.
Played in the wrong way.

Now, that beautiful smile is gone.
Replaced by complaints and frustration.
I hope you find your way.
Forgive me for not guiding you toward it.

scene 89

You treated my heart like a hub station,
A temporary layover until you figured out
Where you were really going.
Then, you were off,
Leaving me in your wake.

Another would stumble in after you were gone,
Dazed, confused, yet captivated
By the warmth and generosity.
But they, too, departed, leaving echoes behind.

I always craved someone to linger,
Roaming the halls, impressed by the archways,
Inclined to stay and listen with feverish intent
To the pulse that keeps everything going.

It felt as if everyone was destined to pass through,
So I strived harder to impress, to compel someone to stay.
I was always the one pleading my worthiness.
I never paused to ponder their depths,
I just yearned to be chosen.

You shuffled your feet, scuffing the floors.
Leaving your imprints inside these walls.
Littered it with your promises to come back and
Your unresolved issues that I am left to resolve
To justify allowing your presence in my life.

scene 90

Maybe it's not love but shared pain that binds us.
Perhaps that's why our connection is so strong.
And why, when I'm happy, I question what's wrong.

Maybe it's not the joy but our mutual suffering
That forms our common ground.
Maybe that's why it's so cold and intense.

I think we love the messed-up parts of ourselves
And embrace each other's chaos.
Cause while our own struggles may be haunting,
at least someone else gets it.

It's not the love, no.
It's all the ugly parts that you don't share as willingly.
We recognize something in the other, the torment, the agony.
It's this that draws us closer.

What I speak, well, you must have a greater capacity
To understand, let alone love.
Everyone seeks the light, but who loves the dark?

scene 91

I'm not looking for another savior
To absolve me of my sins.
The salvation never lasts.
It's like trying to use people
As a means of healing,
Yet never truly mending.

scene 92

Your eyes keep dancing around like lights in my mind,
Following to every fantasy I create to escape you.
The firmness of your embrace
My face planted against your chest,
The hum of your heartbeat,

The touch of your lips on mine,
The way my nerves would race for you,
Sending every inch of my body into a frenzy.
They all need a place to live, a place to go.

So, maybe this will suffice.
And any time I miss you,
I can come back, think of you fondly,
And then leave you behind.

scene 93

Let me set the scene so you understand
The weight of losing you once more.

Picture days of endless storms, even under sunny skies,
Trapped in a cycle of questions and doubt.
Did I say too much, too little?
Was there something you always weren't telling me?
Why did you come back to just leave me all over again?

Lover, friend, safe space to land,
You took it all with you,
Left nothing behind for me.
I want so badly to hate you,
But there's still a part of me that goes,
I still wish it was you and me.

scene 94

What does letting go look like?
Not talking when I feel the impulse to,
Finding ways to distract myself
From the thought of you,
Reminding myself this is for the best.

It comes in waves.
Give yourself a rest.
It comes in waves.
Take a moment to catch your breath.

Drowning out the thoughts hasn't worked.
So, I acknowledge them and let them pass.
In this ending, I'm learning so much about myself.

scene 95

The whole world I created now lies in ruins.
Left to salvage the shattered pieces of my identity,
I must make another that feels like mine.
Even though I am far from whole.

Someone always takes a bit of me with them.
They don't leave a piece behind of their own to replace it.
Leaving me perpetually diminished.
So persistent about keeping others,
But no one ever stays.

Alone now, I confront my decisions,
Navigating the aftermath they've wrought,
Piecing together fragments,
Crafting a new narrative.
(Eventually, cycles end, right?)

scene 96

Home,
What a concept.
After all this time,
I still don't feel like I belong.
I can rest my head, yes.
Savor meals, find pleasure.
My soul, though, it knows
I'm merely grappling with the idea.

No, there's no place that feels like home,
That would require me to feel safe.
I've been on my toes since eleven.
I just became comfortable
With my heels touching the ground
And catching my breath.
Telling myself the other shoe already dropped.

Don't ask me to call anything home.
I can't yet, I'm still learning
It's ok to trust myself.

scene 97

I'm holding the door, looking at their faces.
As they pass through, on to other places.

No one looks me in the eye,
No pleasantries, or "thank you."
Lost in their thoughts, each on their own.
Navigating life's currents, seeking their way.

Always running a race but never ending up
Where they feel they're supposed to be.
The strain of an existence lacking gratitude.

Who wouldn't wear a blank stare, forgo hope?
Except for artists, who find beauty in despair,
Crafting masterpieces from the pain we bear.

So, here I am, holding a way back to solace.
Still waiting for someone to hold the door for me.

scene 98

How many tomorrows do you have to say, "I love you"?
To tell that friend they changed your life?
How many before your name is no longer spoken?
Leaving behind a silence you can't breach?

How many tomorrows
Before you see I was the answer to your search?
How many before you realize the door is shut tight?

What if you knew the number?
Would you do it then?
Would you cast caution to the wind,
Embracing love with abandon?

How many tomorrows before they no longer pick up your call?
No "Talk soon," or even a "Hello."
Would the memory of their tone follow you around like a phantom?
Would you breathe as easily knowing you didn't call back?

How many more tomorrows
Before we realize today is all we have?

scene 99

It's like they need us to make them feel wanted, to make them feel needed, all while they ruin us. And we don't stop, even when it hurts, even when we can feel we've been pushed to the brink cause we're hoping they'll finally be the person we believe them to be deep down, even though all their actions have spoken to the contrary.

scene 100

There has always been someone
To make me feel like I'm not good enough.
Always proclaiming that they are different.
Only to prove they are the same as every rancid former lover.
These harbingers of doom with false love on their lips.

Have I been the architect of my own downfall all along?
It's a tired narrative, worn and weary.

scene 101

I tell myself I'll find it again,
As if I ever really had it in the first place.

I tell myself it's not my fault,
As if I didn't let it hollow me out
And harden my soft spots.

I don't know what it feels like anymore,
The healing of its touch.
I remember when love was just a theory.

scene 102

If I'm being honest,
I was enamored by your confidence,
The way you effortlessly commanded attention,
Turning strangers into friends with ease,
And making each person feel valued.
Your determination to pursue your desires,
And your ability to assert yourself.

To be frank,
All the qualities I admired in you were ones I aspired to possess.
Perhaps I should have focused on cultivating them within myself,
Instead of making you such a big part of my life.

scene 103

It still hurts.
Less now than before,
But there's still an ache for you.
This thirst that has no name,
But every desire to know you.

Could I not have been spared?
Were you that excited to finally
Hold me in your arms?
How could you let go so quickly, then?
My mouth still remembers the earnestness of your passion.

Was that not something?
I didn't just imagine it.
Years of waiting, years of wanting,
Summed up in a simple action.
It was anything but then.
It was magic.

My heart is now somewhere hidden.
She didn't ask you to arrive,
To give hope and then snatch it away.

You're different now.
And so am I.
I'm just pretending.
That I've remained unchanged.

scene 104

What was it like, watching you fall in love with someone else?
In a word, agonizing, at first.
After the possessiveness of you faded
And the impulse to be angry subsided,
I looked at us through clear eyes.

There was nothing left.

We were lacking in kindness with no consideration to spare.
There were no longing looks, no desires simmering.
Our conversations, still endless, now came with
An inevitable punctuation.
We've always been good at talking,
Just not enough to save us from the false narratives
We each created about one another.

I don't have a desire to hate you.
It's the realization that I'm losing a friend.

I will not stand in your way.
That would just be me keeping myself
From what comes next.
You see, I, too, will discover love anew.
I'm simply taking my time,
Trusting that it will find me
Exactly when it's meant to.

scene 105

All at once, it stops.
The lingering in my belly
That would stir at the thought of you . . .
I won't finish that,
I don't want to wake it from its slumber.
My hand no longer reaches for a means to connect with you.
This madness seems long gone, like it never even happened.
My mind doesn't toil over all the details I loved about you.
Like the way your eyes would pull me in
Or the way your lips . . .
Nope, won't go down that road.
I'm almost there.
I can feel it.
Indifference.
I don't hate or love you.
I just don't care anymore.

scene 106

Thank you for your words
And letting me dance among the melodies.
For allowing me to devour your pain,
Mixing it with my own,
Giving way to some form of comfort.
In the lonely hours, you stayed up with me.
As I lay in despair, you crooned me to sleep.
The reason I didn't give in to dark thoughts.
You were hope for me when I didn't have the strength
To create it for myself,
Reassurance to a girl so unsure about her future.
Thank you for the countless times you saved me.

scene 107

I want to look at someone that way again,
With love written on my face
And anticipation brimming in my chest,
Holding back a little for fear
That my feelings are too much, too soon,
Only to find he feels the same way
And is just as scared.

I want to be scared again,
Cause that way I know I have something to lose,
Deep, daily, all-encompassing.

I want to feel that way again.

scene 108

It goes on, you know.
It doesn't stop cause the hurt won't quit.
It doesn't stop cause you don't want to move,
Holding your breath, just trying to make it through
To the next moment.
It doesn't stop cause you don't want to speak his name
And tear asunder so many of the memories.
It doesn't stop, or wait, or freeze
All because you want him to love you again.
It doesn't stop when you realize
It was really all you
Doing what you typically do.

scene 224

You have taught me
The depths of my own love.

There was a time you radiated happiness,
And even though I couldn't call you mine,
I found solace in your bliss.

But life has shifted since then.
I've come to realize
The facade you wore to conceal your pain.

So, let's make a pact:
I can live without being the center of your world
As long as you, one day, let your guard down.

If not, I'll spend my days
Ensuring you understand
How worthy of love you truly are.

You are not just rooted in me.
Loving you is my purpose.

Should you agree,
I'll gracefully step aside.
If not, I will stand
Firmly beside you.

(No matter what you decide,
Just know, I will always choose you.)